Playing Piano with Three Chords

Christmas

Arranged by Robert Schultz

CONTENTS

Playing Piano with Three Chords

Playing Piano with Three Chords is a series written for the late-elementary pianist. It is an introduction to basic chord playing, harmonizing, and hands-together playing.

The contents have been carefully selected to appeal to late-elementary pianists of all ages, and to provide familiar melodies that are well suited to basic harmonization with easy, chord-based accompaniments. Melodies are harmonized with no more than three chords, usually the primary triads (I, IV, V or V7) in easy key signatures.

A diagram of the basic chord progression used in each arrangement is provided at the beginning of the arrangement. In this diagram the chords are presented in block form for preliminary practice—first in root position, then in the inversions used in the arrangement. Chord names are included in each diagram as well as within the arrangement. In addition to block chords, students will be introduced to simple broken-chord accompaniments in several of the arrangements.

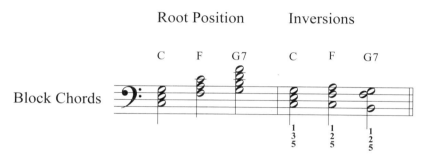

Pieces appear in order of difficulty. The editing is appropriate for the late-elementary pianist, including fundamental dynamics, articulations, phrase marks, and necessary fingering. Every effort has been made to provide high quality, educationally sound arrangements that serve as stepping stones to higher levels while satisfying the student's desire to play popular and familiar music.

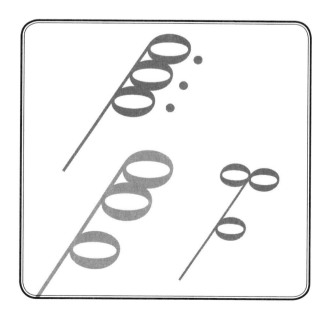

FJH2314

Away in a Manger

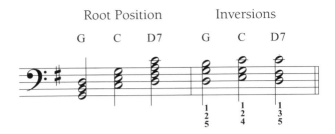

Music by James R. Murray
Lyrics: Traditional
arr. Robert Schultz

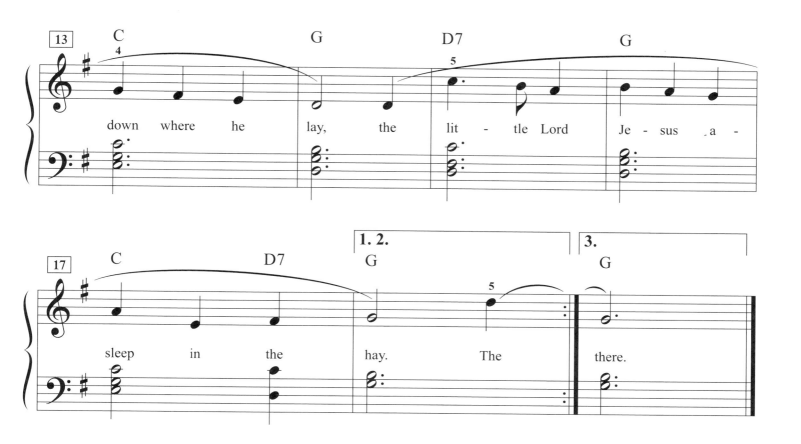

Verse 2:

The cattle are lowing, the Baby awakes,
But little Lord Jesus, no crying He makes.
I love Thee, Lord Jesus; look down from the sky,
And stay by my cradle till morning is nigh.

Verse 3:

Be near me, Lord Jesus; I ask Thee to stay
Close by me forever and love me, I pray.
Bless all the dear children in Thy tender care,
And fit us for heaven, to live with Thee there.

Up On the Housetop

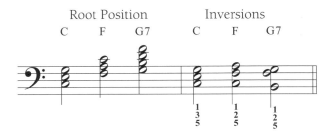

Benjamin R. Hanby
arr. Robert Schultz

Bright and lively

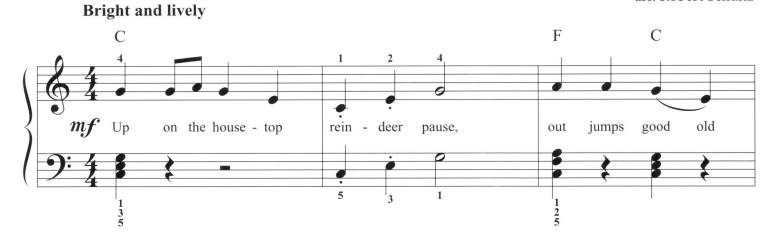

Up on the house-top rein-deer pause, out jumps good old

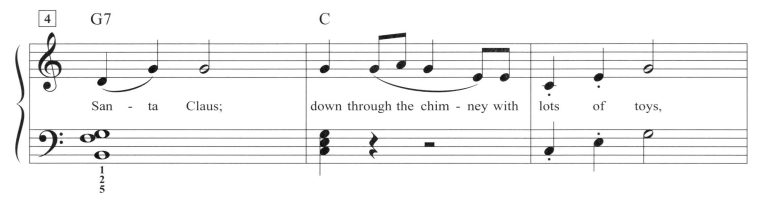

San - ta Claus; down through the chim - ney with lots of toys,

Chorus:

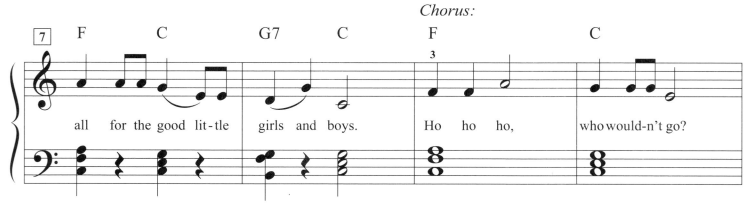

all for the good lit-tle girls and boys. Ho ho ho, who would-n't go?

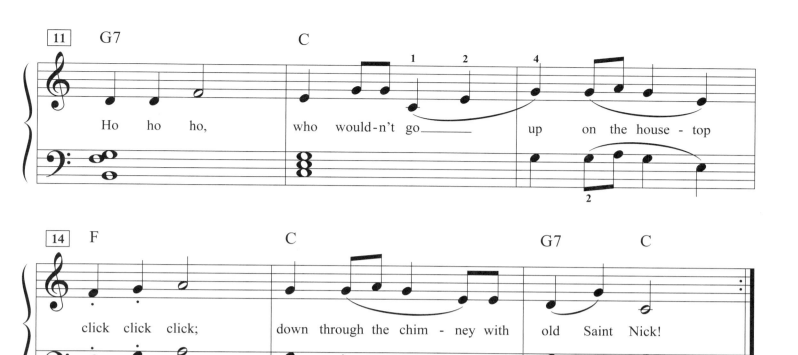

Verse 2:
First comes the stocking of little Nelle;
Oh, dear Santa, fill it well.
Give her a dolly that laughs and cries;
One that will open and shut her eyes.
Chorus:

Verse 3:
Next comes the stocking of little Will;
Oh, just see what a glorious fill.
Here is a hammer and lots of tacks;
Also a ball and a whip that cracks.
Chorus:

The Friendly Beasts

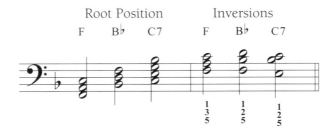

Traditional English
arr. Robert Schultz

Moderately; very flowing

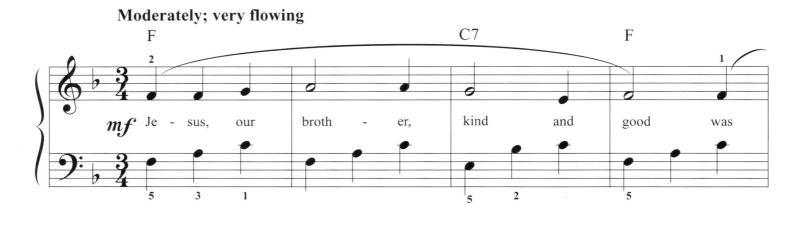

Je - sus, our broth - er, kind and good was

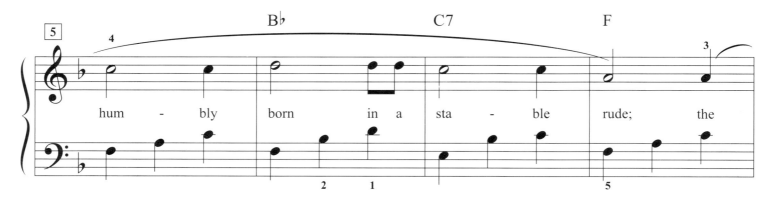

hum - bly born in a sta - ble rude; the

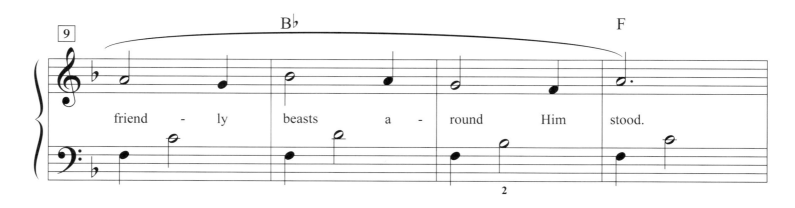

friend - ly beasts a - round Him stood.

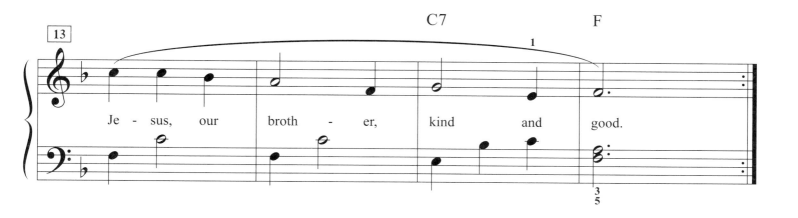

Je - sus, our broth - er, kind and good.

Verse 2:
"I," said the donkey, shaggy and brown,
"I carried His mother up hill and down;
  I carried His mother to Bethlehem town."
"I," said the donkey, shaggy and brown.

Verse 3:
"I," said the cow all white and red,
"I gave Him my manger for His bed;
  I gave Him my hat to pillow His head."
"I," said the cow all white and red.

Verse 4:
"I," said the sheep with the curly horn,
"I gave Him my wool for His blanket warm;
  He wore my coat on Christmas morn."
"I," said the sheep with the curly horn.

Verse 5:
"I," said the dove from the rafters high,
"I cooed Him to sleep that He would not cry;
  We cooed Him to sleep, my mate and I."
"I," said the dove from the rafters high.

Verse 6:
Thus every beast by some good spell,
In the stable dark was glad to tell
Of the gift he gave Emanuel,
The gift he gave Emanuel.

Deck the Halls

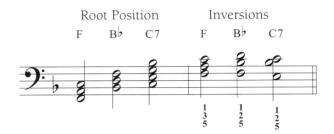

Traditional Welsh Carol
arr. Robert Schultz

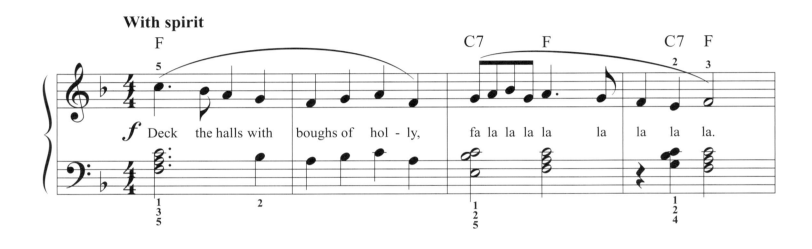

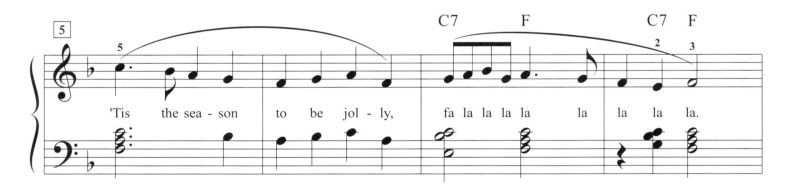

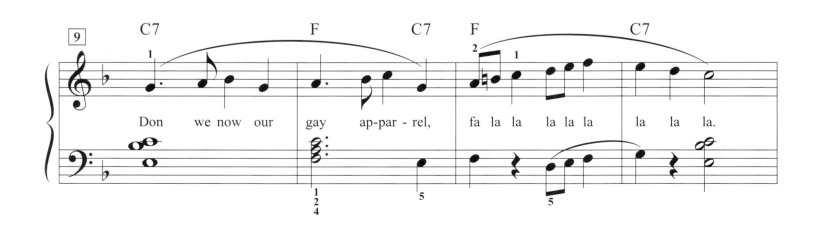

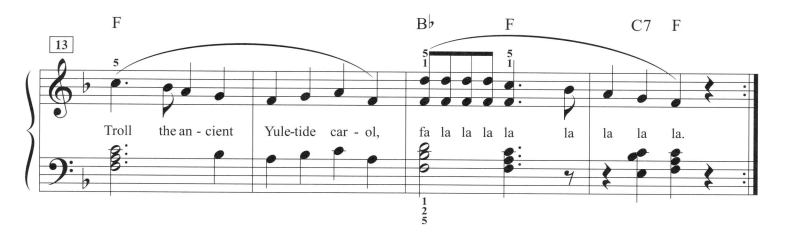

Troll the an - cient Yule-tide car - ol, fa la la la la la la la la.

Verse 2:
See the blazing Yule before us,
Fa la la la la la la la la.
Strike the harp and join the chorus,
Fa la la la la la la la la.
Follow me in merry measure,
Fa la la la la la la la la.
While I tell of Yuletide treasure,
Fa la la la la la la la la.

Verse 3:
Fast away the old year passes,
Fa la la la la la la la la.
Hail the new, ye lads and lasses,
Fa la la la la la la la la.
Sing we joyous, all together,
Fa la la la la la la la la.
Heedless of the wind and weather,
Fa la la la la la la la la.

FJH2314

Between the Ox and the Gray Donkey

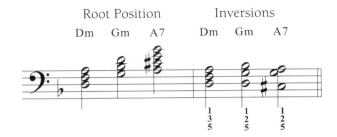

French Carol
arr. Robert Schultz

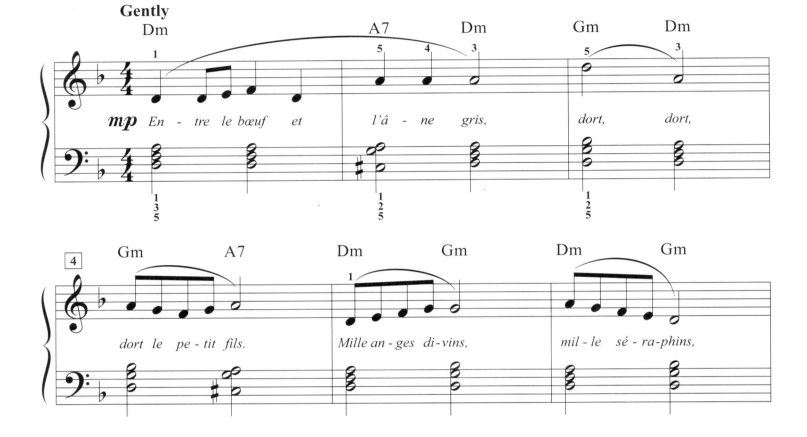

Gently

En - tre le bœuf et l'â - ne gris, dort, dort,

dort le pe - tit fils. Mille an - ges di - vins, mil - le sé - ra - phins,

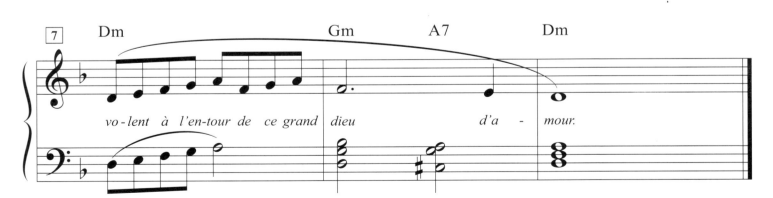

vo - lent à l'en-tour de ce grand dieu d'a - mour.

Between the ox and the gray donkey,
Sleeps, sleeps, sleeps the little son.
A thousand divine angels, a thousand seraphim,
Fly around this great God of love.

Pat-a-Pan

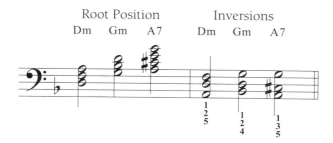

Bernard de la Monnoye
arr. Robert Schultz

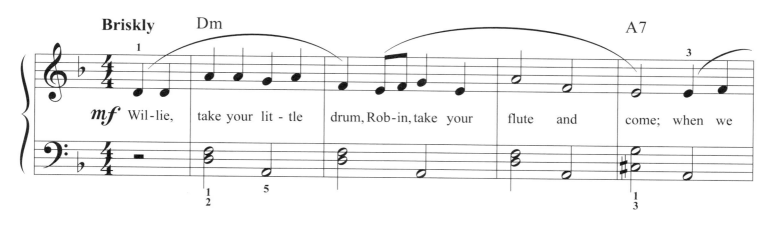

Wil-lie, take your lit-tle drum, Rob-in, take your flute and come; when we

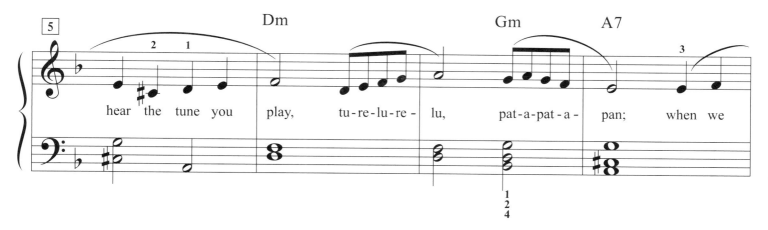

hear the tune you play, tu-re-lu-re-lu, pat-a-pat-a-pan; when we

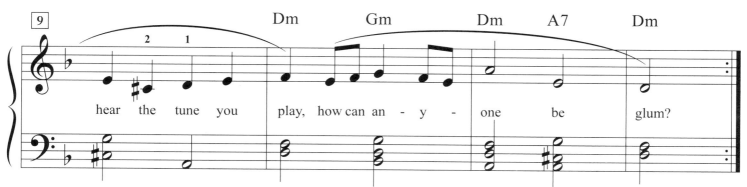

hear the tune you play, how can an-y-one be glum?

Verse 2:
When the men of olden days
Gave the King of Kings their praise,
They had pipes on which to play,
Tu-re-lu-re-lu, pat-a-pat-a-pan;
They had drums on which to play,
Full of joy on Christmas Day.

Verse 3:
God and man this day become
Joined as one with flute and drum;
Let the happy tune play on,
Tu-re-lu-re-lu, pat-a-pat-a-pan;
Flute and drum together play,
As we sing on Christmas Day.

FJH2314

Jingle Bells

James Pierpont
arr. Robert Schultz

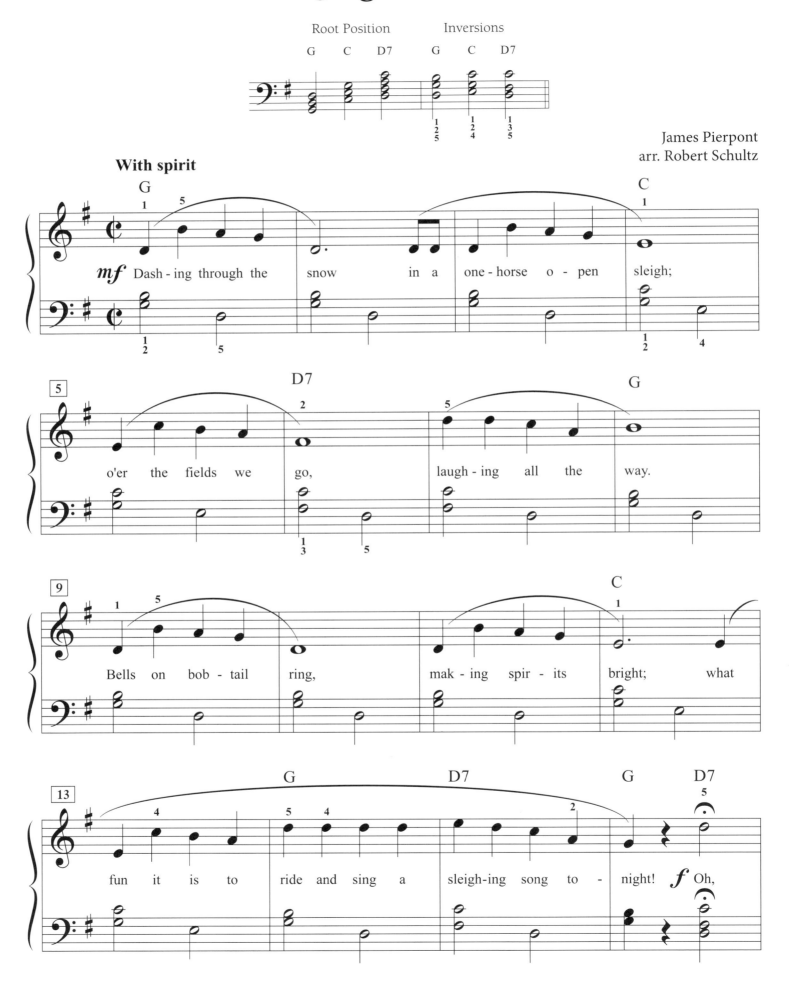

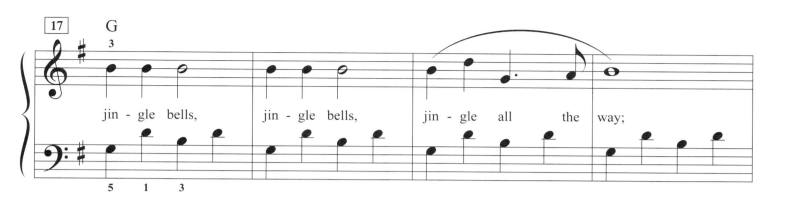

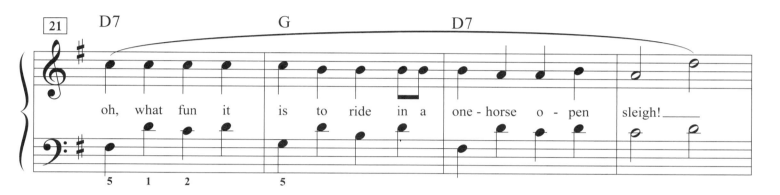

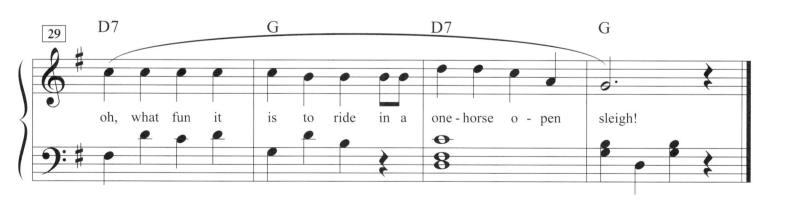

Silent Night

Music by Franz Gruber
Lyrics by Joseph Mohr
arr. Robert Schultz

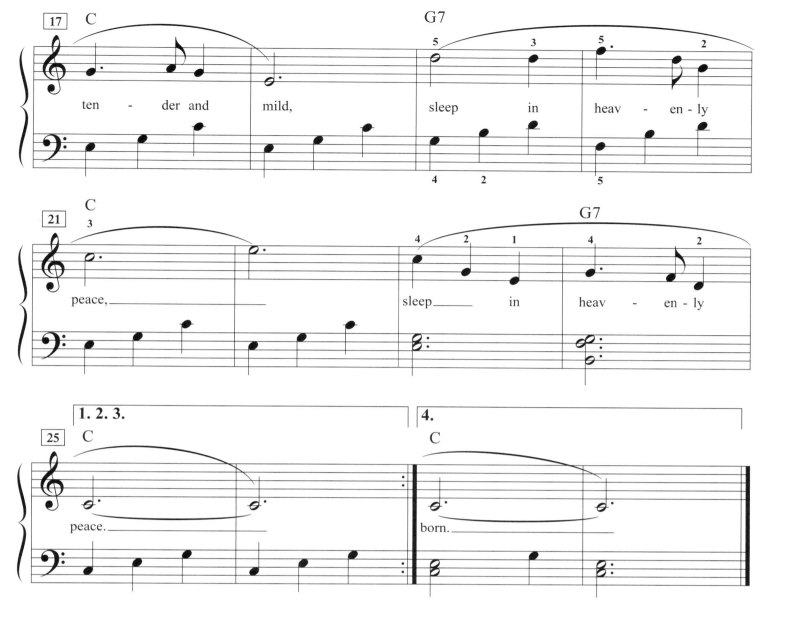

Verse 2:
Silent night, holy night,
Shepherds quake at the sight,
Glories stream from heaven afar,
Heavenly hosts sing Alleluia;
Christ the Saviour is born!
Christ the Saviour is born!

Verse 3:
Silent night, holy night,
Son of God, love's pure light
Radiant beams from Thy holy face,
With the dawn of redeeming grace,
Jesus, Lord, at Thy birth,
Jesus, Lord, at Thy birth.

Verse 4:
Silent night, holy night,
Wondrous star, lend thy light;
With the angels let us sing,
Alleluia to our King:
Christ the Saviour is born,
Christ the Saviour is born.

Good King Wenceslas

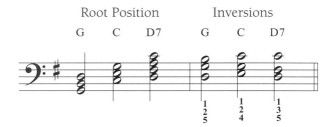

Music: Traditional
Words by John Mason Neale
arr. Robert Schultz

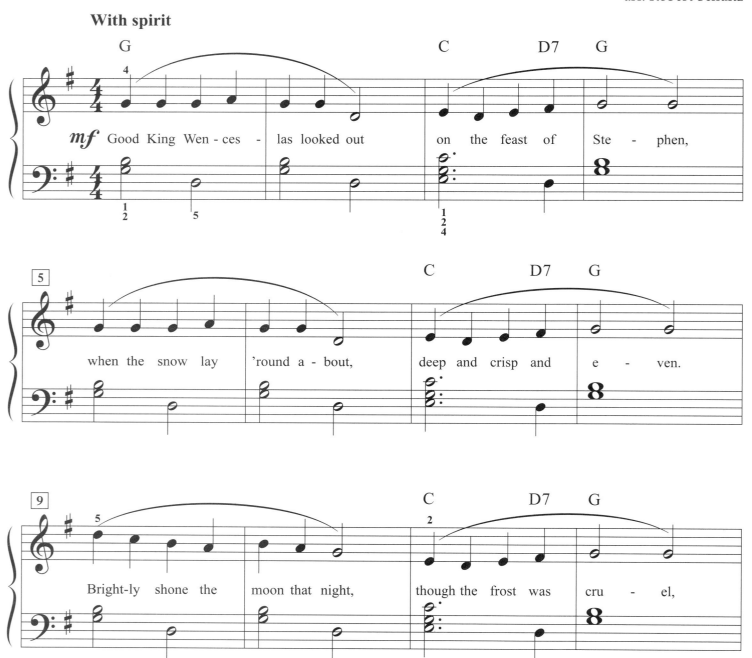

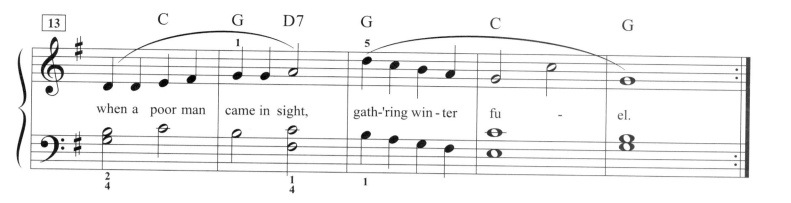

when a poor man | came in sight, | gath-'ring win - ter | fu - | el.

Verse 2:
" Hither, page, and stand by me,
 If though know'st it telling,
 Younder peasant, who is he?
 Where and what his dwelling?"
" Sire, he lives a good league hence,
 Underneath the mountain,
 Right against the forest fence,
 By St. Agnes' fountain."

Verse 3:
" Bring me flesh, and bring me wine,
 Bring me pine logs hither;
 Thou and I will see him dine,
 When we bear them thither."
Page and monarch, forth they went,
Forth they went together;
Through the rude wind's wild lament,
And the bitter weather.

Verse 4:
" Sire, the night is darker now,
 And the wind blows stronger;
 Fails my heart, I know not how;
 I can go no longer."
" Mark my footsteps my good page,
 Tread thou in them boldly;
 Thou shalt find the winter's rage
 Freeze thy blood less coldly."

Verse 5:
In his master's steps he trod,
Where the snow lay dinted;
Heat was in the very sod
Which the Saint had printed.
Therefore, Christian men, be sure,
Wealth or rank possessing,
Ye who now will bless the poor,
Shall yourselves find blessing.

O Christmas Tree
(O Tannenbaum)

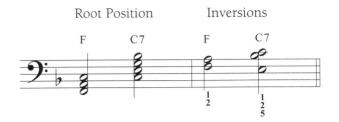

German Folk Song
arr. Robert Schultz

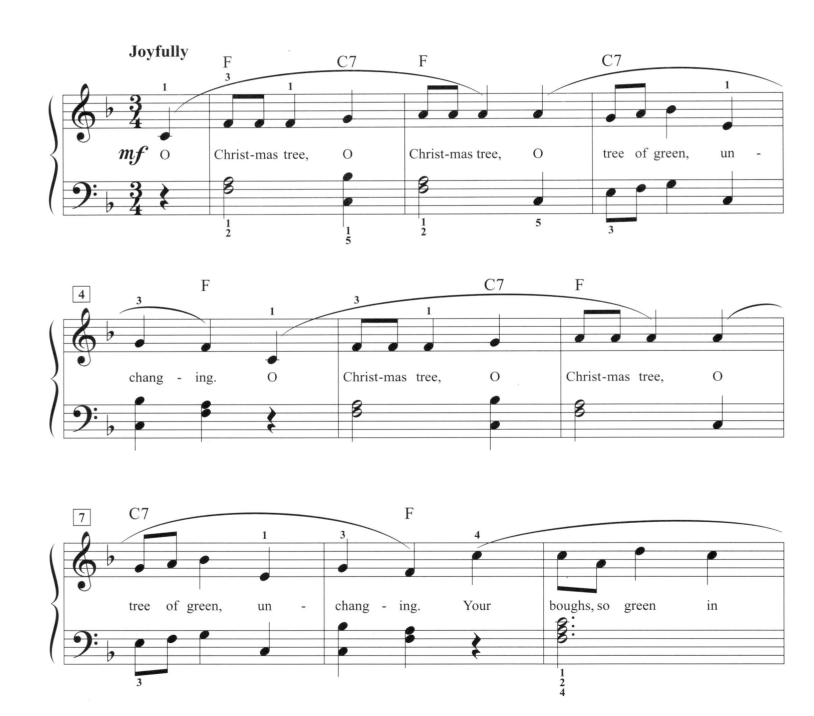

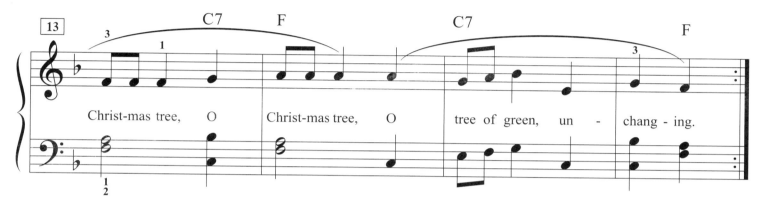

Verse 2:

O Christmas tree, O Christmas tree, you set my heart a-singing. (Repeat)
Like little stars, your candles bright send to the world a wondrous light.
O Christmas tree, O Christmas tree, you set my heart a-singing.

Verse 3:

O Christmas tree, O Christmas tree, you came from God eternal. (Repeat)
A symbol of the Lord of love, whom God to man sent from above.
O Christmas tree, O Christmas tree, you came from God eternal.

Verse 4:

O Christmas tree, O Christmas tree, you speak of God, unchanging. (Repeat)
You tell us all to faithful be, and trust in God eternally.
O Christmas tree, O Christmas tree, you speak of God, unchanging.

Verse 5:

O Christmas tree, O Christmas tree, Thou hast a wondrous message. (Repeat)
Thou dost proclam the Savior's birth, good will to men and peace on earth.
O Christmas tree, O Christmas tree, Thou hast a wondrous message.

O Tannenbaum, O Tannenbaum! wie treu sind deine Blaetter!
O Tannenbaum, O Tannenbaum! wie treu sind deine Blaetter!
Du gruenst nicht nur zur Sommerzeit, nein, auch im Winter, wenn es schneit.
O Tannenbaum, O Tannenbaum! wie treu sind deine Blaetter!

The Snow Lay On the Ground

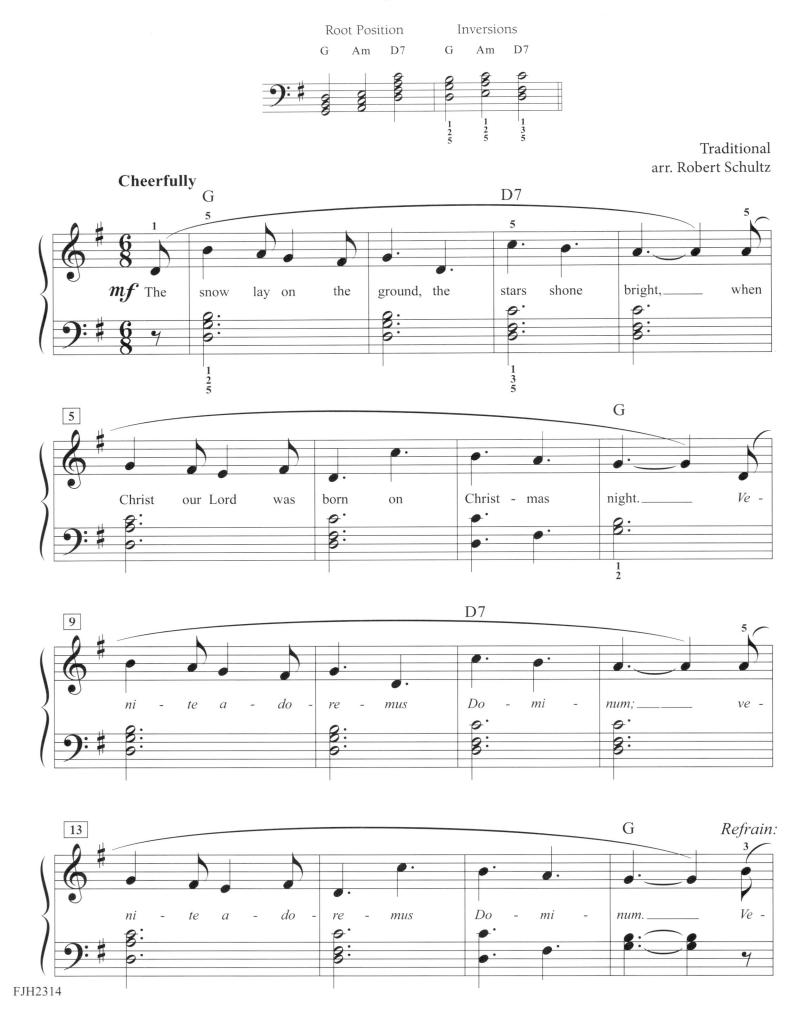

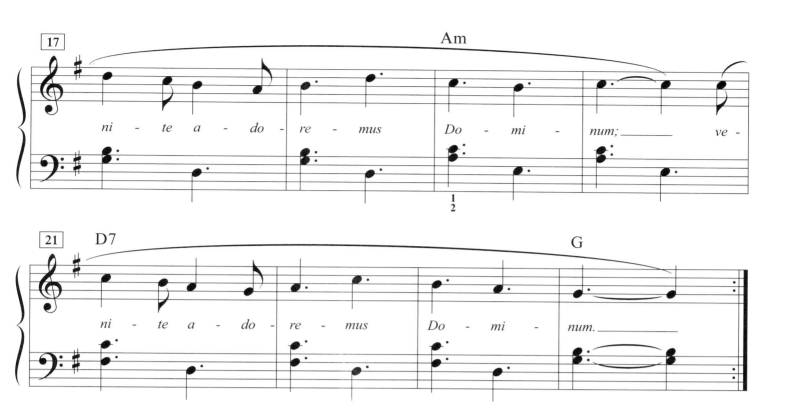

Verse 2:
'Twas Mary, daughter pure of holy Anne,
That brought into this world the God made man.
She laid him in a stall at Bethlehem;
The ass and oxen shared the roof with them.
Refrain:

Verse 3:
Saint Joseph, too, was by to tend the child;
To guard him, and protect his mother mild.
The angels hovered round, and sung this song,
Venite adoremus Dominum.
Refrain:

Verse 4:
And thus that manger poor became a throne;
For he whom Mary bore was God the Son.
O come, then, let us join the heavenly host,
To praise the Father, Son and Holy Ghost.
Refrain:

On Christmas Night All Christians Sing

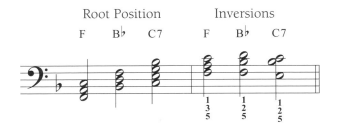

Traditional English Carol
Lyrics by Luke Wadding
arr. Robert Schultz

Moderately; flowing

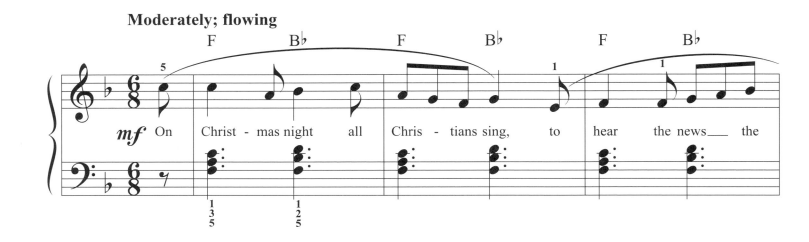

On Christ - mas night all Chris - tians sing, to hear the news___ the

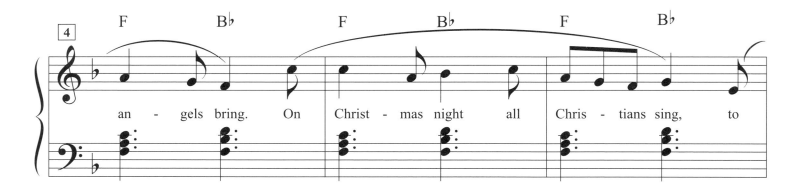

an - gels bring. On Christ - mas night all Chris - tians sing, to

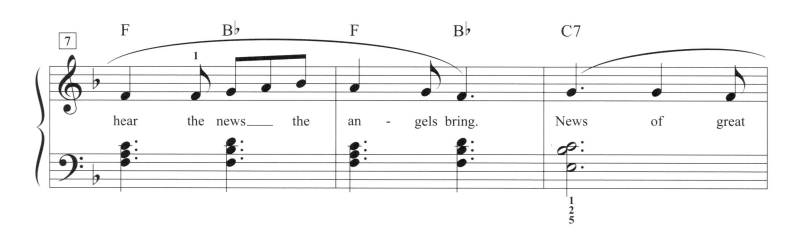

hear the news___ the an - gels bring. News of great

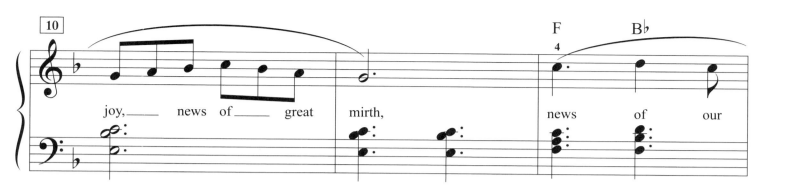

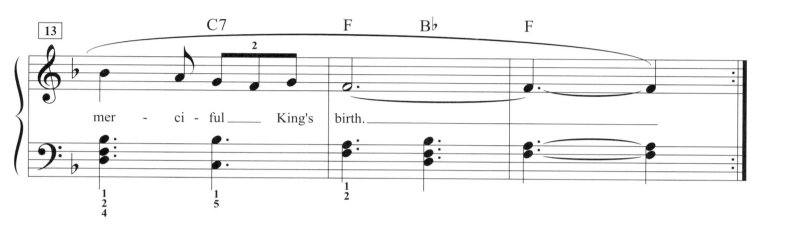

Verse 2:
Then why should men on earth be so sad,
Since our Redeemer made us glad.
Then why should men on earth be so sad,
Since our Redeemer made us glad.
When from our sin He set us free,
All for to gain our liberty.

Verse 3:
When sin departs before His grace,
Then life and health come in its place.
When sin departs before His grace,
Then life and health come in its place.
Angels and men with joy may sing,
All for to see the newborn King.

Joy to the World

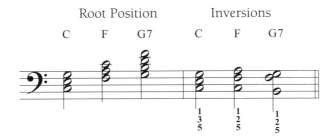

Music by Lowell Mason
Lyrics by Isaac Watts
arr. Robert Schultz

Majestically

Joy to the world! The Lord is come: Let

earth re - ceive her King;_____ Let

ev - 'ry___ heart_____ pre - pare___ Him___ room,_____ and

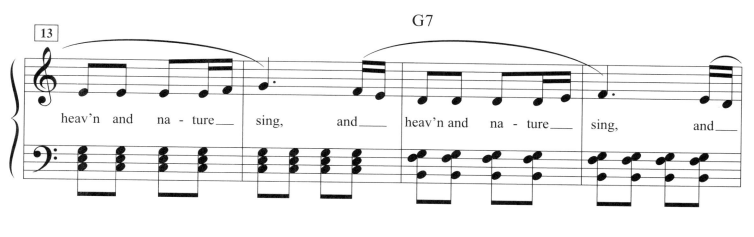

Verse 2:

Joy to the world! the Savior reigns:
Let men their songs employ;
While fields and floods, rocks, hills, and plains
Repeat the sounding joy,
Repeat the sounding joy,
Repeat, repeat the sounding joy.

Verse 3:

No more let sins and sorrows grow,
Nor thorns infest the ground;
He comes to make His blessings flow
Far as the curse is found,
Far as the curse is found,
Far as, far as the curse is found.

Verse 4:

He rules the world with truth and grace,
And makes the nations prove
The glories of His righteousness,
And wonders of His love,
And wonders of His love,
And wonders, wonders of His love.

I Saw Three Ships

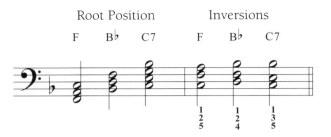

Traditional
arr. Robert Schultz

Cheerfully; flowing

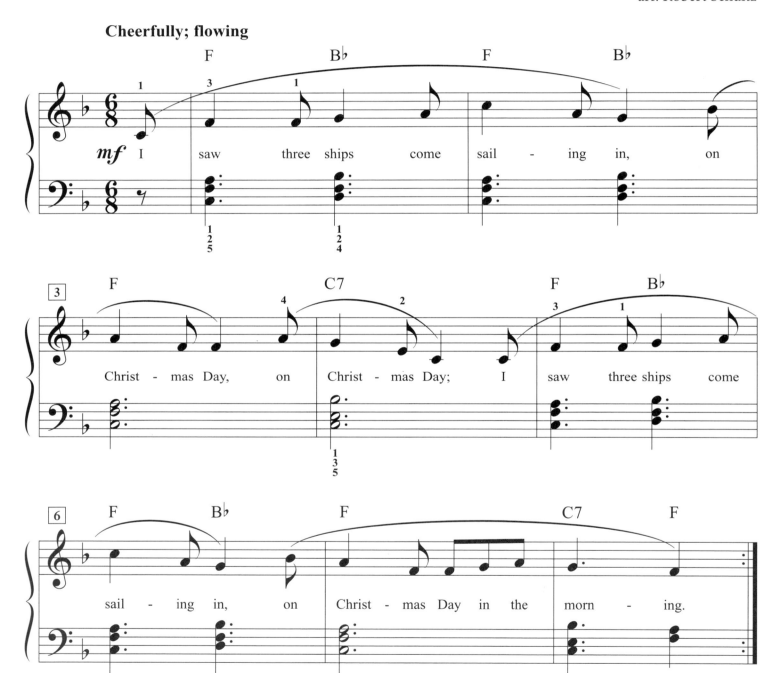

Verse 2:
And what was in those ships all three,
On Christmas Day, on Christmas Day;
And what was in those ships all three,
On Christmas Day in the morning?

Verse 3:
The Virgin Mary and Christ were there,
On Christmas Day, on Christmas Day;
The Virgin Mary and Christ were there,
On Christmas Day in the morning.